News from the North

poems by

Catherine Jagoe

Finishing Line Press
Georgetown, Kentucky

News from the North

ISBN 978-1-62229-816-7 First Edition

ACKNOWLEDGMENTS

My thanks to the following publications, which published earlier versions of these poems:

Poem, "Snapshots"
Verse Wisconsin, "Felicité Petitot"
Flurry, "Epiphany"
Red Wheelbarrow, "Fog's Breath Coheres"
Nebo, "News from the North"
2014 Wisconsin Poets' Calendar, "Thaw"
diode, "Hope" and "North of April"
Red Wheelbarrow, "Green Hummingbird"
qarrtsiluni, "Still, Life" and "Psalm"
Inisfree Poetry Journal, "The Secret Heat of Trees"
Comstock Review, "Bloodroot"
Atlanta Review, "Dog Days" and "Solstice Under Snow"
Sow's Ear Poetry Review, "In the Heartland"
White Pelican Review, "Kite"
River Oak Review, "A Collect for All Saints' Day"
North American Review, "Arctica Islandica"

Editor: Christen Kincaid

Cover Art: Katrin Talbot

Author Photo: Rubén Campos Reyes

Cover Design: Elizabeth Maines

Printed in the USA on acid-free paper.
Order online: www.finishinglinepress.com
also available on amazon.com

Author inquiries and mail orders:
Finishing Line Press
P. O. Box 1626
Georgetown, Kentucky 40324
U. S. A.

Table of Contents

SNAPSHOTS

There's a photograph of me with bleached hair
and a red sweatshirt, holding up a frozen disk
of Tombstone pizza, on a long straight road,
yellow wilderness on either side,
a Badlands wind that made my fingers ache.
I was twenty-six and drunk with possibilities.
We had six days to reach the west coast in a borrowed car,
and we had to stay ahead of the snow.

There's another photograph of me with an elk
blurry in the background. I'm leaning against a sign
that says CANADA 20 MILES, jaunty and smiling,
surrounded by white. We spent that night at a Motel-6,
four of us in two twin beds to save twenty bucks.
I was too paralyzed with awkwardness to sleep.
My Belfast bedmate's complex vowels sounded
again and again in my head like a faulty LP, and I
was hounded by desire that sprang only from proximity,
branded on the hip where our bodies bumped
once in the narrow bed. He kept his back to me.
I thought about his wife, and kept my hands off him.

That was the trip I learned somehow to ski,
in Glacier National Park on a gunmetal grey day.
We paused beside a frozen lake, and he
stripped off his shirt and stood with his thin,
white back bared to the wind that smelled of snow.
That night I felt myself falling,
atom beneath colossal depths of dark.

The storm swept up upon our heels—
we barely made it through the Cascades.
Cars were beached on every side but we,
young and omnipotent, lurched and veered
on upwards through the driving sleet,
drove straight out of winter into spring,

saw snow melt and a man walk by in his shirt sleeves
in the mild air of that Pacific coast.
We steeped in colors at the marketplace,
a carnival of fish and fruit we hadn't seen for months.
I bought a bag of clementines but found
you can't take clementines back home.
I ate them all, there in the airport, every little sun.

FELICITÉ PETITOT, d. DEC. 27, 1856

Wife of a journeyman, she'd survived
it all: the trek across the breadth
of France from her hamlet in the east
to Paris, seething and cacophonous,
and on to the grey sea she'd never seen
either, at Le Havre, the forty-five days
on the ocean, almost being washed
overboard, filth, frostbite, typhus, hunger,
unloaded like freight at Castle Rock
with $12 and her lace-making bobbins,
the paddle steamer up the Hudson River,
trudging in home-made wooden clogs
through the bush, and on again
over the Great Lakes, dreaming all the while
of getting to the place *Wisconsin,*
the eighty acres waiting, full of wild fowl,
deer, trout, mandrake fruit and yellow flag;
the river, woods and upland lush
with butternuts and hazel, blackberries,
violets and grapes; not knowing that air
could be like knives, or that the trip
would take so long; landing in Milwaukee
just before her Christmas birthday, 1856,
fifty-five years old, one hundred fifty miles
to go to reach Belleville, Wisconsin,
by ox-drawn wagon through deep snow,
quailing at the wolves howling at night,
shivering with ague, she rode up top,
the men struggling on foot through drifts.
Just twenty miles from what was
to be their home, the driver hit
a tree stump buried in the snow.
The wagon bucked and pitched
her, headfirst, to the frozen ground.
She'd never live to see the pigeons
thick as swarming bees.

TWELFTH NIGHT

Each year around this time I founder
nightly, snagged on the wrecks of phantom lives.
I am not commuting on the interstate,
driving into the endless heart
of a white chrysanthemum.
I am not all alone in the world:
loverless, childless, friendless.
I am not late to give an exam,
and the exams I have taken are not
still looming, forbidding as Everest.
I do not crash-land on barbed wire.
I make myself heard.

Yet still, each year, the icefishers
with their augers and bright lures
hook me in the dark waters.

The candles snuffed, the presents, litter.
The tree with its scent of memories and need
now stripped of its suit of lights,
dragged out, diminished, Cinderella.
On the radio, a choir sings *Kyrie eleison.*
In the arbor vitae, a lone red cardinal.

FOUND

On the ground outside the grocery store
on Thursday morning, late December,
bleak light and bitter wind hazing
the parking lot, an empty
half-gallon vodka bottle,
its clear, slabbed sides as thick
and colorless as lake ice, radiating
cold. "One hundred proof" it says
of human sorrow. What man or
woman drained this vessel to the last
drop of distilled grief and tossed
it out the window, before or after
loading the week's food in the truck
and driving home to the kids?
Shards of a life, lives,
splintering, smashed upon
hard liquor.

EPIPHANY: JANUARY 6

I wake to a vitreous world
   exquisite, pitiless,
glazed in glare ice
   that sheer veneer

all glitter and crystal
   no green victuals here
winter has seared
   the fat off the land

its maw yawns, yearns
   to maul us, bite
after frosty bite,
   man-eater

it has tasted blood
   last night a sleepwalker
who strayed out barefoot
   died, all blued

and it is stalking me
   I've seen its paw prints
on my windscreen's
   damask, deadly spoor

DOG ON THE MEDIAN OF THE KENNEDY EXPRESSWAY, CHICAGO

I keep coming back
to that dog
running west
next to the fast lane
along the concrete meridian
between eight
lanes of traffic

and wishing
I could have stopped
although it was impossible
four lanes of us
nose to tail
seventy miles an hour

that dog, thin, grey,
loping doggedly along
no Samaritan in sight
nowhere to go but on

FOG'S BREATH COHERES

Imagine—
the radio antenna on my car

has suddenly sprouted
teeth. It has become

a prehistoric twig, bristling with white spines.
The wire fence around the heating plant has grown frost thorns.

Each stem and stalk and looping spray of the trees on the hill
is rimed with tiny hackles, stiffly raised

like the million sensitive feet of the dying starfish
or the inner tentacles of anemones as they dry.

On the corner by the railroad tracks someone appears
to have planted a Walmart's frosted pine.

The grizzled trees float above their trunks
in hazy clouds, like white lichen.

I walk through groves
of pale coral.

HOPE

Valentine's Day: a buzz
around the flowers in the grocery store.
Outside, icy sidewalks, grubby snow.
Young men, mostly, on their lunch-break, hover
over the roses and gerberas.
A woman carries a helium balloon,
exclaiming to her friends, glad
she's found the right thing.
Down the aisle, an old man
hesitates, gripping his cart
with its scant gleanings of bachelor food:
one-serving canned soups, Doritos,
sliced bread. He is unshaven,
unhandsome, dressed like someone
who's never had much.
In his right hand, askew, a lone
red rose in a cellophane holder
like those ruffs they put around dogs
to keep them away
from their wounds.

NEWS FROM THE NORTH

I tell you
how the sunflower seeds
I put out for the starving birds
have started to sprout
where they spilled
on the basement floor
by the pipe that drips
in the dark

I tell you
that our grass is dead
snow-burned and flattened
littered with discards
defrosted dog-shit
a black flashlight
a blue gum wrapper
a child's fuchsia glove

in Catalunya there are almond trees in bloom

you tell me they have sliced
into your breast
cut and cauterized and sewed and iced
to stop the rotten milk that has started to flow
now though your boys are grown

you tell me you have pierced
the skin of leafless trees up north
that clear sap dripped from them
you collected it in pails
boiled it down for hours
sweet boiled maple blood

the lake ice is softening
becoming granulate, absorbing light
starting to glow

THAW

Last night I dreamed
I held a lover in my arms,
drinking the softness of his face,
stroking the hyacinth bud
upon his thigh until it flowered,
warm and wet, in the palm of my hand.

Walking raw and dream-shocked
through dun-greys of late winter,
I suddenly smell the earth. The lake
runs free, slapping the shore, its carapace
dissolved this year in record-making time.
High up in the cottonwoods, a din:
hundreds of male redwing blackbirds,
just arrived, raucous with excitement,
above the swamp they always breed in.

I stand, my face upturned, sensing
the pull of longings and regrets
that well up at the start of every spring.
And then the old knowledge comes to me:
the body mimicking the moon,
a stirring in the clenched fist of the womb.

Already I have heard the courting calls
of great-horned owls,
in the cold woods
at nightfall.

NORTH OF APRIL

the house smells of bought daffodils
grown somewhere south of here
somewhere kinder

I crack the bedroom window
for the first time in five months and forget
to close it

at night freezing we drink
the sweet wine of the day's air

down the street a Muslim gives a Jew a medal
of the Buddha for surviving influenza
and the winter alone with two kids

tulips are thrusting up fistfuls of shoots
not green but red like secret body parts
exposing themselves

a girl is rescued from death by her ponytail
grabbed by her cousins
after falling through thin ice while playing

and today on the marsh a pair of sandhill cranes
with their scarlet caps and big bustles stalk awkwardly
stumbling when the ice gives under them
they raise their heads and cuss the air
when I so much as move

it's the first time I've seen wild cranes so close

I've only ever glimpsed them high and far away
although I always start up when I hear
them calling a rusty hinge creaking
in the wind a door long shut
inching open

STILL, LIFE

the world is warming
the Antarctic ice shelf just lost
a chunk large as Manhattan magnified by seven
if you live in America
my land by emigration

in Britain the land of my birth
that chunk was the Isle of Man

in Spain my land by adoption
it was the province of Burgos

to feel loss we have to make it local
the globe our yard

once as a child I saw a Portuguese man-of-war
drifting downwind mauve caravel
in pristine waters off the Outer Hebrides
but now my humming screen predicts the Gulf
Stream that hugs the British Isles
could stray plunging the kingdom into a new
Ice Age

last year I saw twelve storks trying to nest on one church tower
in old Castile no longer
migrating south to Africa

but winter here on the Great Lakes was so hard the squirrels
gnawed the bark from the small high branches
ice dammed on eaves and melted into ceilings
highways became rutted village lanes
and icicles hazardous to passing humans
mice invaded our basement to steal cat food
which they stored in the oven thereby
setting it on fire

the recently emerged yards
    are muddy as flood-grounds
spring has come violent here
    this week I saw a home lurch
whole and entire   into a brown   maelstrom
    and break apart   roof upside down

        a ruined ark

THE SECRET HEAT OF TREES

After the last, piled snow sublimes
but before the ground's greening,

when dust from the tiller rises
like smoke from the prairie burning,

the naked maples start to drop
their draggled, red litter of buds,

the way a bitch in heat drips rust,
blooming on a single afternoon

when the air turns wanton.
Remember, every tree's a lover.

Even plain old ash, box elder, elm,
oak, yew, boast stamens straining,

anthers opening, pistils soft as dew.
Their sperm dancing on the wind

besieges our moist cavities, inflames
us, causing wheezing, itching, ooze.

Attempting to avoid a ravishment
by trees, we stream, weep, sneeze.

BLOODROOT

Outside the music teacher's house, this
first brownish thrust of live leaf from dead,
this small native ephemeral, so
unlike its primal, sexy name that conjures
phallus, rutting, menses.

Bloodroot is Easter Week, the Paschal lamb,
is Bach and the Passions,
string consorts on their period instruments
wringing sounds from sheep gut,
so like the human voice, with its
consonants and vowels,

bloodroot is bitter myrrh, is torture,
is forsaken, resurrected,
is the waning and waxing
of this world now quickening,

is the house finches returning
expectant, with their complex
liquid song, and the robins'
cheeriup, cheeriup, cheerio,

is box elder bugs making out on the front step,
coyote scat in the park, a rabbit's nest, old
honeycomb in the grass,

is magnolia in bud, a few
musky cream cups leaking their green,
veiled scent,

is the old lady across the road, 102,
whose bridge partner picks her up and drops her off
resplendent, and the ambulance that comes
at times, lights flashing,
but leaves without her,

is the red-garbed cardinal intoning
too, too few, few, few.

GREEN HUMMINGBIRD

I will not forget the summer I forced myself
out onto the deck and slumped there in despair,
swollen-eyed, slatternly, my throat raw,
my head heavy with drugs that made me
endlessly sleep and eat but did not cure my pain,

how you suddenly appeared, suspended
in mid-air, a jeweled messenger
on wings of living, iridescent green.
The ruby at your throat glowed in the sun
as our eyes met. No one else saw you.

I knew your message was yourself: green
flame of concentrated life, scrap of pure
unbounded energy. The next time I labored
under the same weight, you reappeared:
hovering between the lilacs and the bleeding heart.

PSALM

I pause in the airport parking ramp, alive
with the avid conversations of sparrows
honoring the ordinary.

They make this half-deserted hangar
musical as a cathedral, open to the air,
full of light and shadows, cool spaces.

I see our house when it was a great skeleton
of yellow wood, the roof ribs of whale,
green glow of summer in the rafters.

A wasps' nest falls from the heft
of the silver maple. I hold
this fine grey paper from the sky.

I sing, and sometimes sound fills
my mouth and throbs there, my throat
an instrument, my ribs a soundboard.

I swim, keeping my head low
in the water, thinking of seals:
breathe, swivel, drive, flip, glide.

I endure the clamor of children,
ground down smooth by it, like shingle
clattered and worn on the strand.

I plant wormwood and sage.
I snap asparagus spears,
split the wood from the green.

The mock orange that I tried to kill
is drenched in blossom, tipsy.
Again, its scent undoes me.

DOG DAYS

Now comes basil, bosomy, floreted,
come sweat-beads oozing,
comes bee balm rouged and thrumming,
come parch, come drench, come swelter,
come raspberries, comes rainbow chard,
come water lily meadows with their glint-blue sprites,
come oriental knights in bronze and malachite
to filigree the cherry's leaves,
come Sungolds swelling, throngs
of coneflowers massing,
comes flit of lucent lemon finches,
come daylilies' long-legged, sprawling stars,

comes first cicada shell in grass,
comes August sizzling with them sawing;
come cantaloupe and corn-ears,
blowzy, heavy-headed, toppling
over summer's cusp towards the fall.

CYCLING TO BLUE MOUNDS

A high wind hisses
through the corn stalks, stiff
and gaunt as castaways,
rattles the sun-bleached tatters
of their once-fine clothes.
Riding towards the warm eye
of that enormous wind
is squint, lung-burning labor
to make scant headway,
but when it is behind us
there is sudden quiet, as if
it had just died, though we are hurtling
on at thirty miles an hour.
At each turn in the road
the crosswind hits us,
snatches our breath, blinds us,
whips us to exhilaration.
We plunge and crest,
loving this land, black
earth, soy fields, red barns,
surfing the massive
rollers of the hills.
Deafened like sailors
we wheel and plane
over the surging earth.

IN THE HEARTLAND

It is homecoming season, Ironman season,
wasp and Concord grape season.
It is seed-head season for turkey foot and little bluestem,
season of dying Black-Eyed Susans.
Katydids' season to rasp like hooligans with wooden rattles.
It is gourd and beet season, hip and haw,
hickory and walnut, muskmelon and mushroom.
Starlings' season to mill in the burning bush,
swallows' to twitter on telephone wires.
Season of rot and wither and drop,
of topple and windfall, of riot and wishbones, of drab and flame,
season of apples and honey, of awe and atonement,
of sun-wane and night-spill, of last times.
It is squirreling season, season of grubs and peeling and gales,
of canker and worm, of frilled purple kale,
of boarding up and closing down, of silent summerhouses,
of storm windows and choked gutters, screen storing, rakes and piles,
season of soups and cider, of Nyquil, of fleece and fingerless gloves,
season of disguises, season of dread, decay, decline,
of ripe and relinquish, of scour and rage, of hog-fattening,
of falling silent, turning in, of closing doors,
of knuckles, of ebb and resignation.
It is red-osier dogwood fruiting season.
It is the season of striped woolly bears on roads.
It is aster and clotted snakeroot floweret season, silk of milk-
weed glistening, season of split pods,
of muskrat prints paddled from mire to boardwalk
through the cattails, of cranberries and corn mazes,
of school buses, of whetting,
of whistle blasts on fields and chants and teams drilling,
of stadiums roaring like rising jets,
like the sound of a distant, deep-throated sea.

KITE

You fell in love with it at Ace Hardware,
tawdry plastic triangle emblazoned
with a Warner Brothers bear whirling
up out of a tornado, arms akimbo, all snarling
teeth and huge pink tongue. We balked
at the price, $3.59 for a flimsy sheet of plastic,
four dowels the size of straws, a cord
as thin as sewing thread. With your small boy
yen for things flamboyant and cartoon
you begged for it, adamant, so we paid up
and went to fly it.
                                        The riot wind
felt good, warm enough for shorts,
too strong for wasps, mosquitos, no-see-'ums.
In the park, the urgent cries of soccer teams,
children shrieking on the slide. I was bored,
drained, wishing I could sleep, released
from mothering. Wisps of cirrus
overhead, banked storm clouds moving in.
You wanted to let it out as far as it would go
and you were right. Low down it kept on veering
into nose dives, tangling with trees, but at a hundred yards
the current started, unseen high road.
The kite sensed it, child yearning at a gate
to another world. Up there it came alive,
giant tiger moth, quivering, eager, wild.
We passed it back
                                        and forth, you and I,
lying by the lake behind the ice-cream store.
Earth and wind, grass and cloud, ground and sky.
It felt like fishing, braced against such strength,
the kite anchored on the wind, straining
to leave, yet steady at its distance, tethered
for now, like you to me, like both of us
to earth.

A COLLECT FOR ALL SAINTS' DAY

November 1, for all saints and martyrs,
known and unknown

Geese work the shorn field
that just last week bore corn,
gleaning the combine's leavings:
stray, stripped red cobs, chaff,
husks, kernels in the dirt.

Remember, they can be found.
The poor find them.
Sometimes odd grains
are all we have.

And sometimes abundance
is laid waste or despoiled.
Fauré scraped by on a pittance
while his publisher's wife
snipped his songs to circles
to cover her pots of jam.

Machado held his mother on his lap
in the truck jolting over the Pyrenees
to exile; queued at the French border
with only his rain-soaked suit and the cold
that would kill him. Without
the suitcase of unpublished work
the soldiers said they'd forward.
Dying, days later, in January '39
he wrote: "These blue days
and this sun of childhood."

An ailing writer in my town says
each day he's like Odysseus.
As he arises, his feet,
like the hero's, shine.

Thoreau, in the last days before he died,
asked what he could glimpse
of the other side, said gently,
"One world at a time."

SOLSTICE UNDER SNOW

December guttering almost to the wick.
The houses shawled, the shrubs white sheaves,
and phantom knives ranged neatly on the eaves.
At pewter dusk, a giant low is wending
east towards us, bearing more snow.
You kiss me goodnight, retire to read
by lamp-light, sip molten peat.
Waking warm in night's long deep,
furled in our feather bed, I know
the snow's slow silt is drifting down,
sifting the buildings with silence up to the sills.
Our house is shingled tight.
Lulled on the steady swell and ebb,
the softly breaking waves of breath—
yours, mine, the cat's—I feel
a coal shift somewhere, suddenly,
and flare, a sudden blaze
of glad to be your kith and kin,
spliced, hitched, in this for life.

ARCTICA ISLANDICA

1.
Seeing the ice, congealing like white fat
on the dark stock of the pond, I think
of the four-hundred-and-five-year-old clam
just dredged from the Arctic Ocean
north of Iceland. Quahog *Arctica Islandica*,
the oldest living creature ever found,
born the year the English encountered Cape Cod
and William Shakespeare wrote *Othello*,
three when *Don Quijote* hit the press,
seven when Galileo peered through
his first-ever telescope. In those cold
and pristine seas it drifted, larval, landed
upon velvet silt and burrowed in,
growing a film of shell a year. Daily
it sipped a slow rain of plankton.
Global warming researchers from Wales
sawed unsuspecting through its small,
drab and unremarkable shell to tell
its age, counting its rings like a tree's.
An unfortunate aspect of our work
was that the clam died.

2.
I once worked eight years in the deep
mid-west at a job I hated in a town known only
for the invention of barbed wire and GM corn.
The Chicago and Northwestern Railroad ran
right through it. Freight trains
would wake me at ungodly hours, wailing
like banshees, long into the seamy night,
shaking the floorboards and the raddled
window sashes in the clapboard houses.

3.
The last glacier of the last
Ice Age passed through the city
where I live, scouring all beneath.
Just west of here, it stopped.
The country beyond has hilltops,
views, variety, a sense of perspective.
To us the glacier left the shriven plain,
the sand and clay I wrestle with
each summer, planting annuals.
Ten thousand years have passed
and still, this far north, winter
is a spiritual exercise, weight-
training for the soul.

4.
The Roto-Rooter Man tries doggedly
but fails to fix the trammeled drain.
He blames it on the trees,
their greedy roots. Sober
for twelve years, he says
he's gone back to the drink.
Was it the blizzard? I think,
the freezing rain?
Too many drains?
After that visit he vanishes,
answers no more calls.

5.
My son, five, wants to know
why God, who could choose to make us
live forever, lets us die.
It's not kind of him, he reasons, puzzled,
beginning to be aggrieved.

6.
I know Tylenol and temperatures and loose teeth.
I know mounds of corn snow and blebbed ice.
I know whitegreybrown.
I know Christmas lights
in the dark. I know
chapped lips.

7.
A ten-year-old in Mexico
glues his hand to the bedstead
after Christmas, not wanting
the humdrum life of school.

8.
That clam and I have things in common:
the drabness of our lives,
the cold, the hidden muscle.
I am reminded of him when the snows
keep falling and I weep over onions,
endlessly load the dishwasher,
endlessly wipe the counters with a dirty cloth,
do endless laundry and find underpants
and fix holes in knees. As I clean
cat vomit and hairballs.
Contemplate my small living room
endlessly choked by toys.

I know thickened.
I know a slowed heart.
I know hunger expanding.

9.
I want marigolds and mangoes.
I want lambs keeping me awake
with their bawling and celandines
on the airfields and the valleys opening.
I want woods full of bluebells.
I want the mountains of North Wales:
Moel Siabod, Cadair Idris, Tryfan.

I want figs and custard apples.
I want thyme on the hillsides
and lemons on the trees.
I want to go back to that place in Spain
called "Birth of the River World."

I want a Welsh men's choir
with a thunderous golden organ
to fell me, belting out "Cwm Rhondda"
like the crowds at rugby matches:
Bread of Heaven, Bread of Heaven,
Feed me till I want no more (want no more)
Feed me till I want no more.

10.
I open and inhale saffron, desiring
everything to be yellow, orange, red.
All winter, I cook foods from abroad.
Fry olive oil, turmeric and sweet paprika,
sweat shallots. I cook basmati,
brown rice, purple, white. Roast squash
in oil of French hazelnuts
till carmelized. Grate ginger root.
Split green cardamom, pour
coconut milk. Chop feta cheese
and dill. Simmer broth
of miso, shiitake, kelp.

11.
I listen to the shipping forecast
for the British Isles:
Dogger, Fisher, Viking, German Bite,
Rockall, Shannon, Fastnet, Lundy,
Irish Sea. South wind veering west later,
gale force eight, occasional showers, rain.

12.
Growing up near Wales, I never listened
to Welsh men's choirs. I only noticed
how barren and poor the life was:
the rain on slate roofs, slag heaps,
the mountains bleak and shrouded.
I never noticed with what joy
they could sing of hardship,
ordinariness, endurance.

I never expected
happiness, *pilgrim*
in this barren land.
This barren, rich life.
Our unremarkable existences
with their secret, iridescent insides.

ADDITIONAL THANKS

I am grateful to the Money For Women/Barbara Deming Memorial Fund for a grant that made it possible for me to be a Day Fellow at Edenfred artists' residence in Madison, Wisconsin in 2009, and to David Wells and the Terry Family Foundation for creating a peaceful space to write there.

My thanks to Jerry Remy for his generous help with the history of early French settlers in Belleville, Wisconsin, which led to the poem on p. 3.

Catherine Jagoe is a writer and translator specializing in Spanish and Catalan. She has a PhD in Spanish literature from the University of Cambridge and is the author of a book of literary criticism, *Ambiguous Angels: Gender in the Novels of Galdós* (University of California Press, 1994). Her translations include the Amnesty International award-winning Argentine novel *My Name is Light* by Elsa Osorio (Bloomsbury, 2003) and *That Bringas Woman* by the nineteenth-century Spanish novelist Benito Pérez Galdós (Everyman, 1996).

Poems from her first chapbook *Casting Off* (Parallel Press, 2007) were featured on *The Writer's Almanac* and *Poetry Daily*. Her poetry and essays have appeared in numerous journals, such as *Gettysburg Review, Chautauqua, American Athenaeum, Contemporary American Voices, North American Review, Ninth Letter,* and *Atlanta Review*.

Originally from the UK, she now lives in Madison, Wisconsin, with her husband and son. She is a contributor to Wisconsin Public Radio's *Wisconsin Life* series. For further information, please visit www.catherinejagoe.com.